26504455

9/0r

Crafts to Celebrate

God's Creation

Crafts
to Celebrate
God's
Creation

By Kathy Ross
Illustrated by Sharon Lane Holm

The Millbrook Press
Brookfield, Connecticut

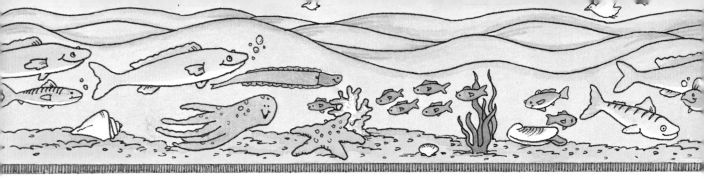

To my loving and supportive extended family
at Gethsemane Church, Sherrill, NY
K.R.

For Pat and Merial, thank you!
S.L.H.

With special thanks to Patti M. Hummel and the Benchmark Group

0-7613-1621-3 (lib. bdg.)
0-7613-1330-3 (pbk.)

The Library of Congress Control Number: 00-039413

Published by The Millbrook Press, Inc.
2 Old New Milford Road
Brookfield, Connecticut 06804
www.millbrookpress.com

Contents

Introduction

The crafts in this book provide a way to help children become more aware of God's amazing creation. They are based on Genesis I:1- the recounting story of God's creation, the world and its inhabitants.

Beginning with the world itself and all of its wonderful and diverse physical attributes, the crafts follow the Genesis story through the creation of birds, beasts, and fish, culminating in the creation of the first people. These hands-on crafts will encourage reflection on God's creation.

The final projects are reminders of God's great love for the world He has created and, more specifically, each person in it. The book ends, most appropriately, with a project of thankfulness and praise to God who gives us such great gifts.

Kathy Ross

God made the earth that we live on.

Glue and Tissue Earth

you need:

white tissue paper

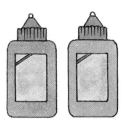

blue and green
colored craft glue

pin

wire or string

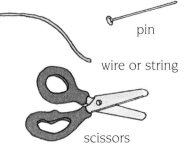

scissors

Styrofoam tray to work on

what you do:

1 Cut two 1-foot-square (30-cm) pieces of tissue paper.
Place them on the Styrofoam tray.

2 Squeeze a 5-inch (13-cm) circle of blue glue onto the
paper. Fill in the circle with blue glue. This will be the
water on the earth.

3 Squeeze some green glue over the blue glue down the center of the earth for landforms.

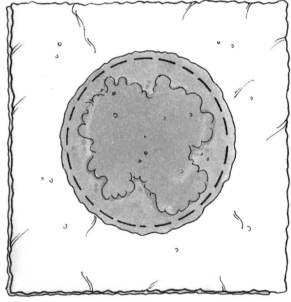

4 Carefully set the second square of tissue over the glue earth on the first square of tissue. Let the glue dry completely. This can take several days. After a couple of days, if you have sealed pockets of glue, poke the pockets in two or three places with a pin so that the air can get in to dry the glue.

5 When the glue has dried completely, cut out the earth in a circle, using a small plate or bowl as a pattern. Trim away any rough edges of glue.

6 Poke a hole in the top of the earth with the pin or the end of the wire. Thread wire or string through the hole and twist or tie the ends together to make a hanger for the earth.

This project looks especially pretty hanging in a window with the sun shining through it.

Thank you, God, for our earth.

God turns the night to day.

Night to Day Wheel

you need:

two 9-inch (23-cm) uncoated paper plates

black and blue poster paints plus two other colors

paintbrush

yellow construction paper

sticker stars

white glue

scissors

fiberfill

yarn, doilies, and other collage materials

paper fastener

what you do:

1 Cut a window about 3 inches (8 cm) tall and 4 inches (10 cm) wide in the top half of one of the paper plates.

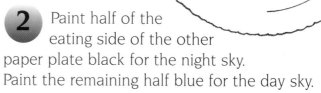

2 Paint half of the eating side of the other paper plate black for the night sky. Paint the remaining half blue for the day sky.

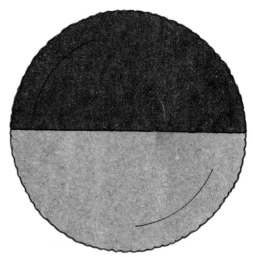

3 Cut a 1 1/2-inch (3.75-cm) circle from the yellow construction paper. This will be the moon. Glue it in the night sky, making sure it will be visible through the window cut in the top plate. Glue sticker stars around the moon. Use glue, even though the stars are self-stick, so that they will not rub off when turning the sky from night to day.

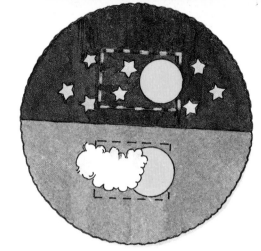

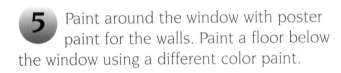

4 Cut a 2-inch (5-cm) circle from the yellow paper for the sun. Glue the sun on the blue-sky portion of the plate, making sure it will be visible through the window cut in the top plate. Glue some wisps of fiberfill over one side of the sun for the clouds.

5 Paint around the window with poster paint for the walls. Paint a floor below the window using a different color paint.

6 Use the yarn, doilies, and other collage materials to decorate the "room."

7 Place the window plate over the sky plate and fasten them together with a paper fastener through the center of the two plates.

To change the night to day, just turn the back plate around to show the day sky.

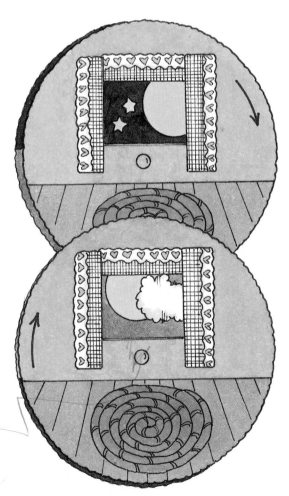

Thank you, God, for the night to rest and the day to learn more about your love.

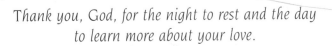

God put the sky over the earth.

Sky Puppet

you need:

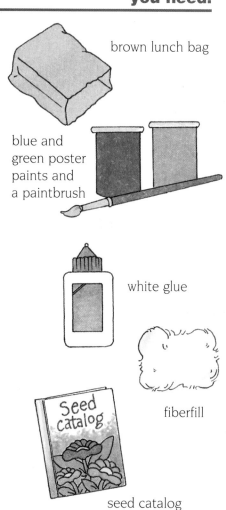

brown lunch bag

blue and green poster paints and a paintbrush

white glue

fiberfill

seed catalog

scissors

what you do:

1 Work with the bag upside-down and the folded bottom of the bag on top.

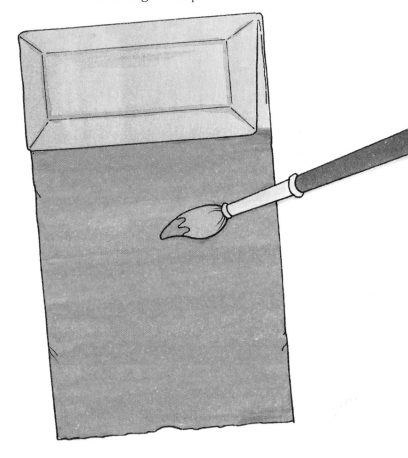

2 Paint the part of the bag below the edge of the bag bottom green for the grass.

3 Open the fold of the bottom of the bag and paint it blue for the sky. Let the paint dry.

4 Glue a wisp of fiberfill in the sky for a cloud.

5 Cut flower pictures from the seed catalog. Glue the flowers on the grass.

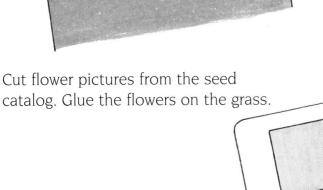

To use the puppet slip your hand into the bag with your fingers bent over the fold in the bottom of the bag. When you tell someone that God made the sky, open the bottom of the bag to reveal the beautiful blue sky that is over the earth.

Thank you, God, for the sky above us.

God made the sun in the sky.

Sunrise Cup Puppet

you need:

9-ounce (266-mll) disposable cup

coffee filter

watercolors

yellow poster paint

paintbrush

stapler

orange pipe cleaner

11/2 -inch (3.75-cm) Styrofoam ball

craft stick

white glue

scissors

Styrofoam tray to work on

what you do:

1 Trim the top off the cup so that it is about 2 1/2 inches (6.5 cm) tall.

2 Cut the coffee filter in half. Save the other half for another project. Slide the flat side of the cut filter into the cup and trim it so that it forms an arch sticking up out of the back and sides of the cup.

3 Working on the Styrofoam tray, paint the filter all over with patches of watercolor. Cover the filter with a thin layer of glue to stiffen it. Let the filter dry on the Styrofoam tray.

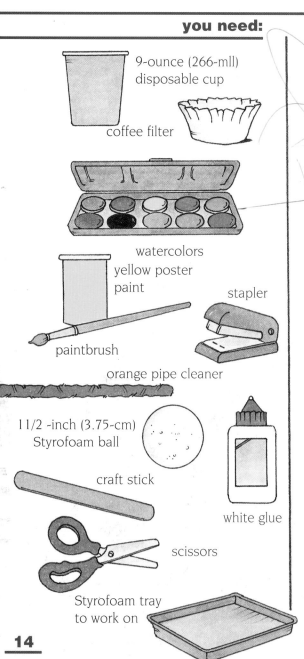

4 Staple the filter to the cup.

5 Paint the Styrofoam ball yellow for the sun. Cut 3/4-inch (2-cm)- long pieces of orange pipe cleaner to stick around the ball for the rays of the sun.

6 Push the craft stick into the bottom of the sun. Pull the stick out, cover the end with glue, and put it back in.

7 Poke a hole through the bottom of the cup. Drop the end of the craft stick down through the hole so that the sun is hidden in the cup and only the beautiful colors of the sky above the horizon are visible.

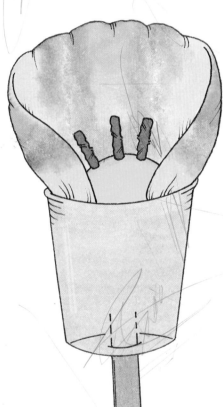

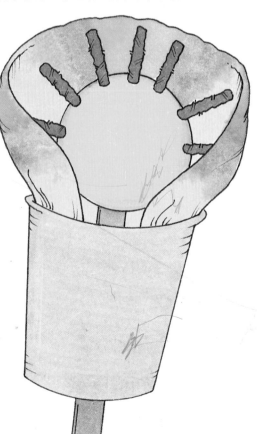

You can make your sun rise by pushing on the end of the stick at the bottom of the cup.

Thank you, God, for the sun that comes up every morning.

God made the moon that shines
in the night sky.

The Changing Moon

you need:

round lid from
a cookie tin

yellow tissue
paper

pencil

ribbon

white glue

masking tape

black
construction
paper

sticky-back
magnet strip

scissors

what you do:

1 Use the pencil to trace around the lid
on the yellow tissue paper. Cut the
traced circle out. Glue the circle inside the
lid for the moon.

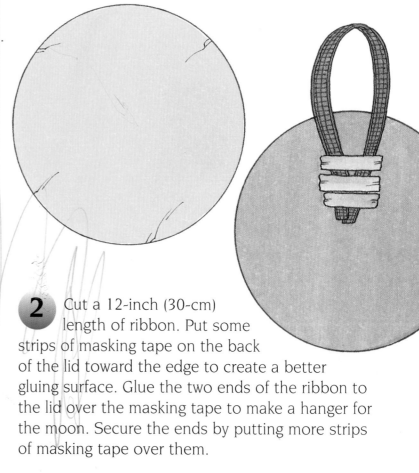

2 Cut a 12-inch (30-cm)
length of ribbon. Put some
strips of masking tape on the back
of the lid toward the edge to create a better
gluing surface. Glue the two ends of the ribbon to
the lid over the masking tape to make a hanger for
the moon. Secure the ends by putting more strips
of masking tape over them.

3 The size of the moon changes as it goes through a cycle. It goes from being completely covered by the earth's shadow to a full circle, then gets smaller and smaller again until it is gone from view. Use the pencil to trace around the lid on the black paper. Cut out three black circles. Leave one circle whole to completely cover the moon. Put a piece of sticky-back magnet on the back of the circle. Cut another circle in half and put a piece of magnet on the back of one half. Cut a sliver of circle from the last circle and put a piece of magnet on the back of each piece.

Watch the moon each night as it goes from a full yellow circle to nothing and back to a full circle again. As the moon gets smaller, you can shadow the right side of your own moon model with more and more black paper. As it gets bigger again, turn the shadows around to shadow less and less of the left side of the moon. You can make lots more shadows in between these sizes or just change the shadow on your moon every few days as you notice a similar change in the size of the moon. What an amazing plan God has!

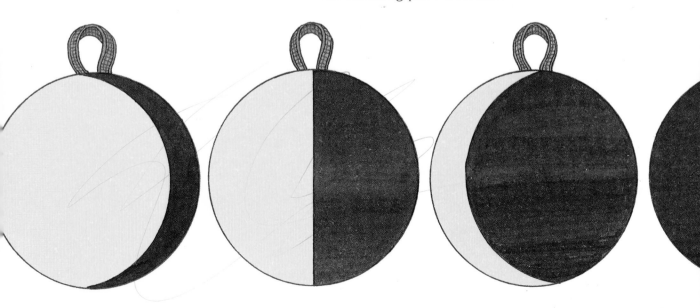

Thank you, God, for the moon.

Star Hair Snaps

you need:

size number 1/0 snaps

sticker stars

masking tape

white glue

tinsel strands

scissors

Styrofoam tray to work on

what you do:

1 Cover the flat topside of a snap with a tiny piece of masking tape to create a better gluing surface. Glue a sticker star over the tape on the snap.

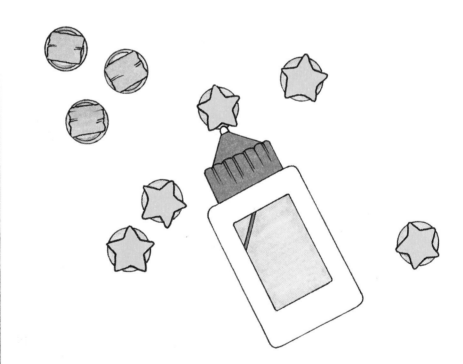

2 Give some of the hair snaps long "tails" by gluing a few strands of tinsel on the tape before gluing the star on.

3 Let the glued stars dry completely on the Styrofoam tray before you wear them.

Make a whole set of these pretty hair snaps. The stars can be worn by snapping the front and the back of each snap together over a few strands of hair.

Thank you, God, for the stars in the sky.

God covered the earth with water.

Water Covering the Earth

you need:

12- by 18-inch (30- by 46-cm) construction paper, 2 black and 1 brown

stapler

sticker stars

glitter

white glue

blue plastic wrap

paper reinforcers

hole punch

yarn

scissors

what you do:

1 Cut a 5-inch (13-cm) circle out of the center of one of the sheets of black paper. This will be for the earth. Staple the two sheets of black paper together along the top and bottom edges, with the sheet with the hole cut in it on top.

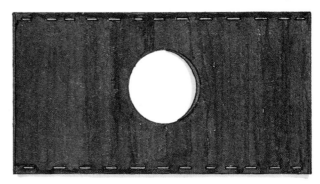

2 Glue sticker stars and glitter on the paper around the hole to look like outer space.

3 Staple a 6-inch (15-cm)-wide strip of blue plastic wrap to the left side of the brown paper. This will be the water. Fold the top and bottom edges of the brown paper up 1 inch (2.5 cm) and use staples to secure the folds. Punch a hole in the center of the left edge of the brown paper. Secure the hole with a paper reinforcer. Cut a 2-foot (60-cm) length of yarn. String one end of the yarn through the hole and tie the two ends together.

4 Leaving 6 inches (15 cm) of brown paper to the left of the plastic wrap, trim off the rest of the right side of the brown paper. Punch a hole in the center of the right side of the paper. Secure it with a hole reinforcer. Cut a second 2-foot length of yarn. String the end through the hole and tie the two ends together.

5 Slide the brown paper in between the two pieces of the black paper so that the blue plastic wrap is hidden on the left and the brown paper shows through the hole. The yarn ties should stick out on each side to pull. Staple the sides of the black paper together above and below the ties.

Show the earth being covered with water by pulling on the right tie to bring the blue plastic wrap into sight.

Thank you, God, for giving us water.

God brought the dry land up
out of the water.

Dry Land Appearing

12- by 18-inch (30- by 60-cm) sheet of light-blue construction paper

stapler

white glue

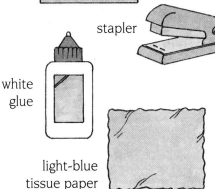

light-blue tissue paper

brown construction paper

straw

scissors

what you do:

1 Fold up about 6 inches (15 cm) of the short side of the blue construction paper. Staple the sides of the fold to make a pocket. Cover the outside of the fold with glue. Then crumple a piece of blue tissue paper into the glue to make the water. Just keep pushing the tissue into the glue until it fits over the folded area exactly.

2 Cut a small triangle-shaped piece out of the bottom of the fold.

3 From the brown construction paper, cut a mountain-shaped piece that is small enough to hide behind the water. This will be the dry land.

4 Staple the dry land to the end of the straw. Slip the other end of the straw into the pocket and cut out the piece from the bottom of the pocket so that the land is hidden behind the water.

Make the dry land appear by pushing on the bottom of the straw.

Thank you, God, for the dry land.

Grass Hat

you need:

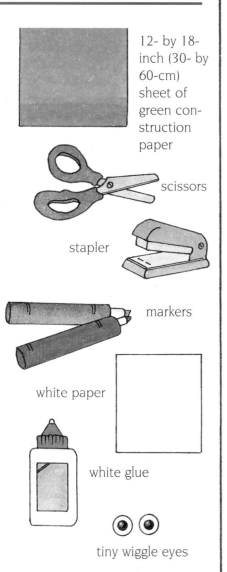

12- by 18-inch (30- by 60-cm) sheet of green construction paper

scissors

stapler

markers

white paper

white glue

tiny wiggle eyes

what you do:

1 Fold the green construction paper in half lengthwise. Cut the paper in half along the fold. Fold the two strips in half lengthwise.

2 Staple the two strips together to make one long strip. Wrap the paper strip around your head and trim off any extra paper from the strip.

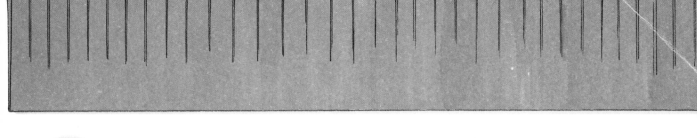

3 Cut fringe all along the open end of the two sides of the folded strip to look like grass. Do not cut through the fold. Staple the two ends of the band together to make a hatband.

4 Use the markers on the white paper to draw little bugs and crawly things to live in the grass. Cut out the bugs. Glue a tiny wiggle eye on each one.

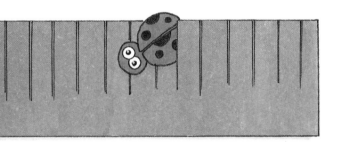

5 Tuck the bugs in the grass around the hatband and hold them in place with glue.

You might want to write "God made the grass" across the bottom front of the hatband.

Thank you, God, for the green grass.

God made trees to grow
on the dry land.

Tree With Squirrel Puppet

you need:

scissors

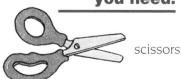

cardboard
toilet-tissue
tube

brown and green
tissue paper

white glue

black permanent
marker

brown marker top

what you do:

1 Cut a 1-inch (2.5-cm) hole out of the side of the bottom part of the tube. This will be the hole for the squirrel.

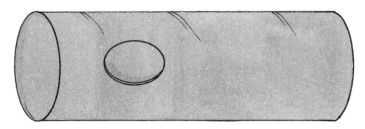

2 Cover the tube with glue, then wrap it in brown tissue paper. The tissue should not be put on smoothly, but with lots of bumps and wrinkles to look like real tree bark.

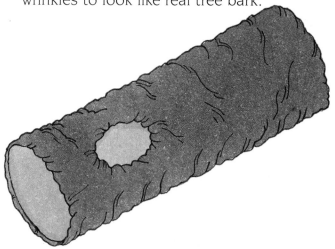

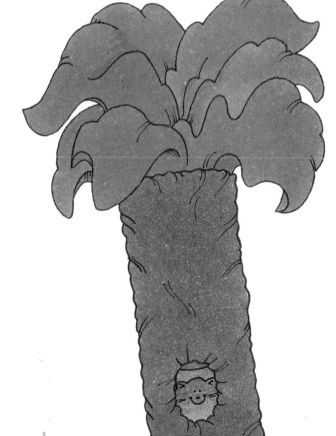

3 Cut three 6-inch (15-cm) square pieces of green tissue paper. Stack them with the corners all going in different directions. Cover the inside of the top of the tree tube with glue. Push the center portion of the green squares down into the treetop so that the green sticks out around the tree for leaves.

4 Use the black marker to draw a squirrel face, paws, and tail on the brown marker top, with the head at the top of the cap.

Put the squirrel on your finger and stick it up through the bottom of the tree to peek out the hole.

Thank you, God, for the trees.

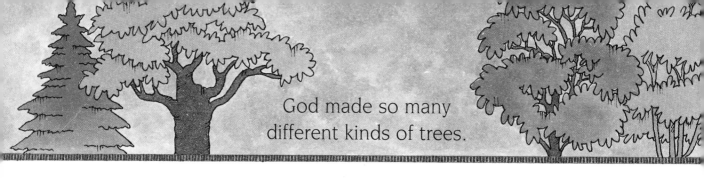

God made so many different kinds of trees.

Spaghetti Tree Pin

you need:

two strands of dry spaghetti

white glue

green glitter

masking tape

pin back

Styrofoam tray to work on

what you do:

1 Break off four 11/4-inch (3-cm) pieces of spaghetti for the trunk of the tree. Glue the pieces together side-by-side on the Styrofoam tray. Cover the pieces with more glue.

2 Break off more pieces of spaghetti of different lengths to make the branches of the tree. Glue them to the tray above the trunk. Cover the branches with more glue.

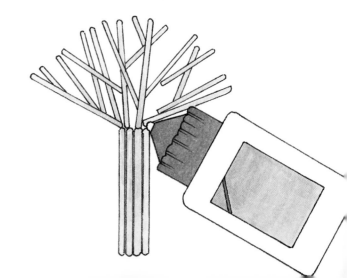

3 Sprinkle the branches with green glitter to look like leaves. Let the tree dry completely on the Styrofoam tray.

4 Wrap the back of the pin back in masking tape to create a better gluing surface. Glue the pin to the back of the tree.

You can wear this tree pin yourself or give it to someone for a gift.

Thank you, God, for giving us so many different kinds of trees.

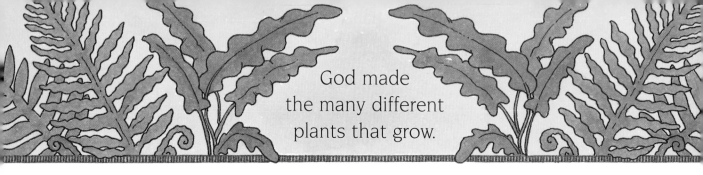

God made
the many different
plants that grow.

Growing Plant

you need:

old stretchy
knit glove

green poster paint

paintbrush

white
glue

stapler

brown
construction
paper

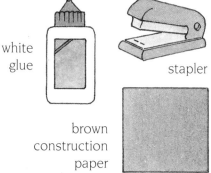

trims

scissors

Styrofoam tray
to work on

what you do:

1 If the glove is not already green, paint its entire outside green and let it dry on the Styrofoam tray. You do not need to paint the cuff of the glove because it will not show.

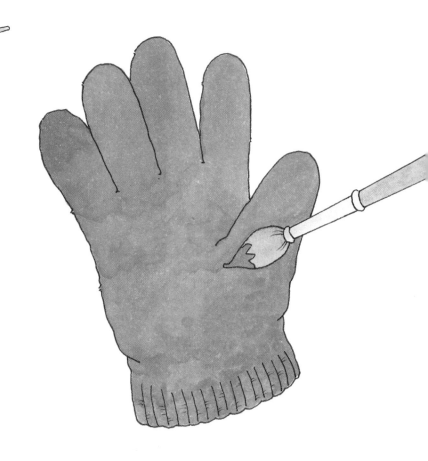

2 Fold the construction paper in half. Starting at the fold, cut a flowerpot shape that is at least 6 inches (15 cm) wide at the bottom and 6 inches tall. Cut along the bottom fold of the pot so you have a front and back piece. Staple the two pieces together along the two sides of the pot.

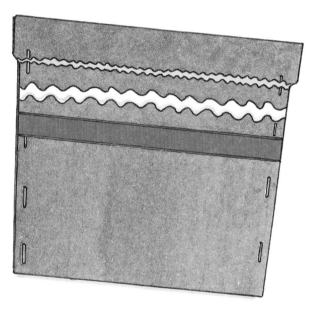

3 Decorate the paper pot by gluing on rows of pretty trim.

To use the plant puppet, put the green glove on your hand and then slip your hand up in the bottom of the pot. Make the plant "grow" by slowly pushing the glove up through the top of the pot.

Thank you, God, for the plants that grow.

God made flowers.

Growing Flower Puppet

you need:

shoebox lid

green and blue
poster paint and
a paintbrush

green and blue yarn

markers

white paper

white glue

masking
tape

scissors

old adult
sock with
stretchy cuff

fiberfill

PRESS

newspaper
to work on

what you do:

1 Turn the box lid so that a short side is on the bottom. Paint the inside of the box lid blue.

2 Cut pieces of blue and green yarn that are about 2 inches (5 cm) longer than the height of the box lid. Tie the ends of the two colors of yarn together to make one long piece.

3 Poke a hole in the center inner edge of the lid at the top and the bottom. String the blue end of the yarn up through the bottom hole and out the back of the top hole. The knot should be in the middle of the box with the green yarn below the blue yarn. Tie the ends of the yarn together in the back of the lid.

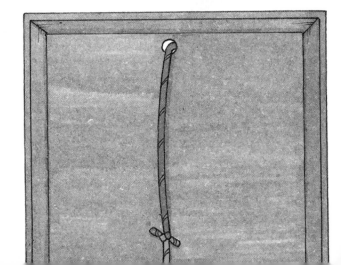

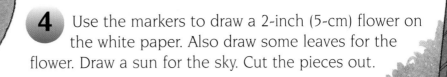

4 Use the markers to draw a 2-inch (5-cm) flower on the white paper. Also draw some leaves for the flower. Draw a sun for the sky. Cut the pieces out.

5 Glue the flower over the knot where the two different color yarns are tied together. Use masking tape to hold the flower in place while the glue dries. Glue the leaves on the green yarn below the flower. Secure the leaves with masking tape.

6 Glue the sun in the sky. Glue some wisps of fiberfill in the sky to look like clouds.

7 Cut a 5-inch (13-cm) band of cuff off the top of the sock. Pull the sock cuff over the bottom of the lid for the ground. If the cuff is not already green, paint the front and sides with the green poster paint.

To use the flower puppet, pull the yarn loop at the back of the lid up to hide the flower in the "ground." Make the flower "grow" by slowly pulling down on the yarn loop.

Thank you, God, for the flowers that grow.

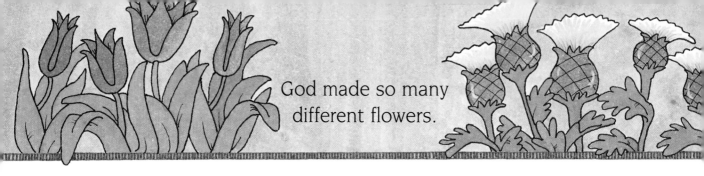

God made so many different flowers.

Handprints Garden

 light-green and dark-green poster paint and a paintbrush

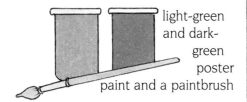 12- by 18-inch (30- by 46-cm) sheet of light-blue construction paper

 old seed catalog

white glue

 old greeting cards with pictures of flowers and insects

 scissors

newspaper to work on

what you do:

1 Paint the inside of your left hand dark green. Spread your fingers and make three handprints across the lower part of the blue construction paper. You will need to repaint your hand for each print.

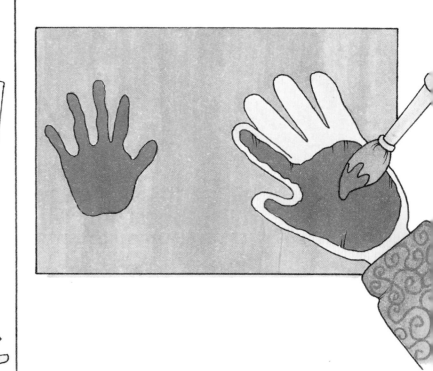

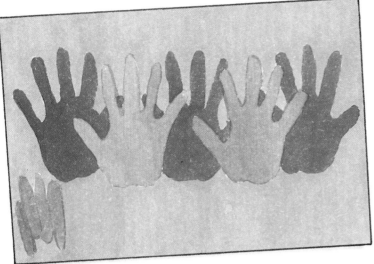

2 Paint your right hand light green. Make two handprints between the dark-green ones. It is fine to have the fingers of the prints overlap.

3 Use your painted fingers to print grass at the base of the handprints in a combination of both shades of green.

4 Cut flower heads for the tip of each finger from the seed catalog and the greeting cards. Cut insects to fly in the space over the flowers and to crawl in the grass below them. When you are happy with the arrangement of your garden, glue the flowers and insects in place.

You might want to write across the top of your garden:
"God made the flowers."

Thank you, God, for all the beautiful flowers

Flying Bird

you need:

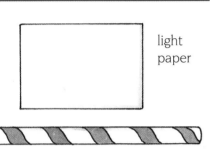

light paper

plastic straw

cellophane tape

scissors

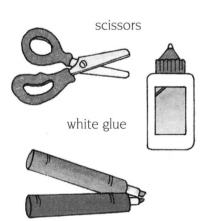

white glue

markers

feather fluffs

what you do:

1 Cut a 4- by 2-inch (10- by 5-cm) piece of paper. Roll the paper loosely around one end of the straw and secure with tape. It must be able to slip easily off the straw.

Slip the roll off the straw and fold the end into a

2 point. Secure the point with tape if you need to. The lighter the bird the farther it will fly, so use as little tape as possible.

3 Use markers to color a beak on the point and draw on eyes.

4 Glue on two small feather fluffs for wings. Add some snips of feather to the back of the bird for the tail.

To fly the bird, slide the bird over the end of the straw. Aim the bird skyward and blow hard in the other end of the straw.

Thank you, God, for the birds.

God made so many
different kinds of birds!

Necktie Bird Finger Puppet

you need:

old necktie

white glue

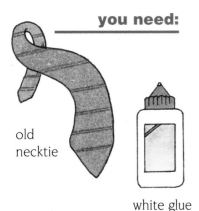
two small wiggle eyes

felt scraps

craft feather

scissors

what you do:

1 Cut a 4-inch (10-cm) piece off the thin end of a necktie. If the seam has come undone in the back, glue it back together.

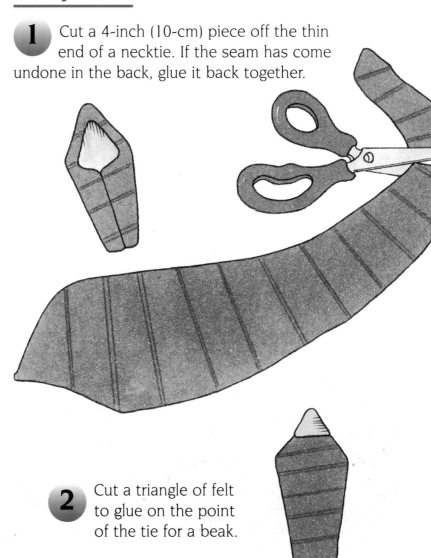

2 Cut a triangle of felt to glue on the point of the tie for a beak.

3 Glue on two eyes above the beak.

4 Fold a piece of felt in half and cut a wing shape on the fold. Open the folded felt so you have two identical wings attached at the center. Glue the center of the wings across the bird.

5 Glue a feather sticking off the back of the bird for a tail.

Make a whole flock of different color birds . . . one for each finger!

Thank you, God, for so many different birds.

Bottom of the Sea Diorama

you need:

disposable plastic container with green or blue top

pipe cleaners

masking tape

gold glitter

scissors

white glue

tiny wiggle eyes

buttons

cellophane tape

shredded cellophane or paper grass

tiny black beads

thread

what you do:

1 Cut a 3-inch (8-cm) piece of green pipe cleaner. Wrap smaller pieces of pipe cleaner around the pipe cleaner piece to make a seaweed plant. Bend an inch of the bottom of the plant to the side and use masking tape to secure it to the bottom of the container.

2 Cover the bottom of the inside of the container with glue. Sprinkle the glue with gold glitter to look like the sandy ocean bottom.

3 Glue some grass to one side of the container for a different kind of seaweed.

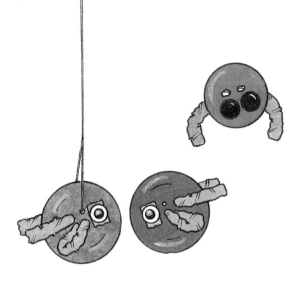

4 Make a tiny crab by stringing the two ends of a 2-inch (5-cm) pipe cleaner piece down through two holes of a button. Bend the two ends forward for the claws of the crab and trim off any extra. Put a tiny piece of masking tape on top of the crab to create a better gluing surface. Glue on two small black beads for eyes. Tuck the crab in among the grass seaweed at the bottom of the container.

5 Use a four-hole button to make each fish. Push a 2-inch (5-cm) piece of pipe cleaner through a hole in the button and fold it in on each side to form fins. Thread a second 2-inch piece through another hole and bend toward the back to make a tail. Put a tiny piece of masking tape on each side of the fish to create a better gluing surface for the wiggle eyes. Glue a tiny wiggle eye on each side of the fish.

6 Cut a 5-inch (13-cm) length of thread. Thread it through a top hole in the fish and tie it to the fish. Use cellophane tape to tape the ends of the thread to the inside of the lid so that, when it is put on the container, the fish hangs down freely, not touching the bottom of the container. Trim off any extra thread. You might want to make more than one fish.

Snap the lid on the container, and your ocean scene is ready to display.

Thank you, God, for all the creatures you put in the waters.

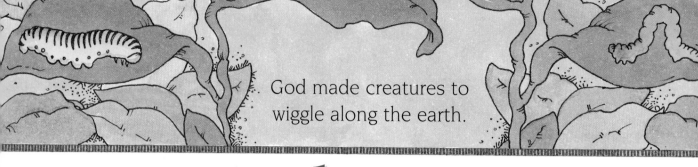

God made creatures to wiggle along the earth.

Wiggle Worm Apple House

you need:

old or unwanted compact disc (CD)

red, green, and brown construction paper

white glue

masking tape

washable black marker

scissors

what you do:

1 Trace around the disc on the red paper. Cut out the circle.

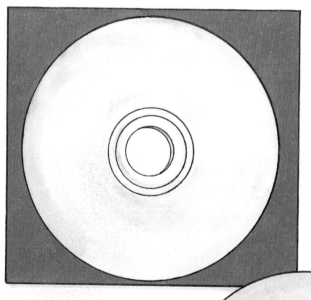

2 Cover the printed side of the disc with strips of masking tape to create a better gluing surface. Glue the red paper circle over the disc.

GREATEST HITS!

3 Use the marker to poke through the paper over the hole in the center of the disc. Trim around the hole with scissors.

4 Cut a leaf for the apple from the green paper. Cut a stem for the apple from the brown paper. Glue the stem and leaf to the edge of the disc to make the top part of the apple.

To use this apple house, you will first need a worm. Use the marker to draw a little face on the end of your pointer finger. If you have a large pointer finger that will not fit through the hole, try your pinkie finger. Stick the little face through the hole and wiggle it around.

Thank you, God, for all the things that wiggle along the earth.

God made lots of little things
that creep, crawl, and fly.

Caterpillar on a Leaf

you need:

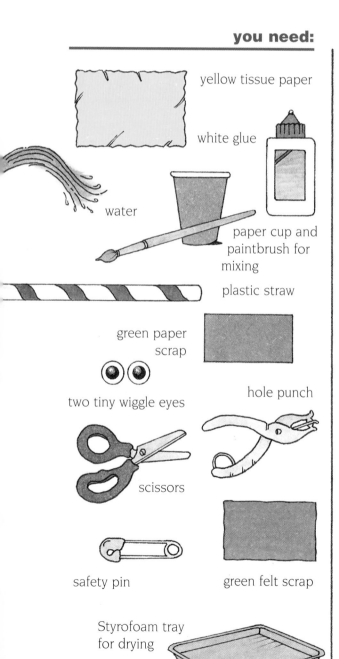

yellow tissue paper

white glue

water

paper cup and paintbrush for mixing

plastic straw

green paper scrap

two tiny wiggle eyes

hole punch

scissors

safety pin

green felt scrap

Styrofoam tray for drying

what you do:

1 Cut a strip of tissue paper 7 inches (18 cm) long and 2 inches (5 cm) wide.

2 Mix a small amount of glue with the same amount of water in the paper cup.

3 Working on the Styrofoam tray, use the paintbrush to cover the strip of tissue with watery glue. Roll the wet tissue around the plastic straw. Carefully slide the tissue paper together along the straw to make the segments of the caterpillar. Work from both ends of the tissue paper until the paper caterpillar is about 1 1/2 inches (3.75 cm) long.

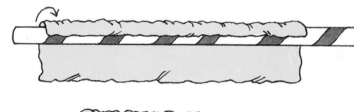

4 Carefully slide the caterpillar off the straw and snap it in the position you want it to dry. Let it dry completely on the Styrofoam tray. It will be hard when it dries.

5 Punch circles from the green paper. Glue the circles along the back of the caterpillar for spots. Glue two tiny wiggle eyes to one end of the caterpillar.

6 Cut a leaf shape from the green felt. Glue the caterpillar to the leaf shape.

You can display the caterpillar flat or add a safety pin to wear it as a lapel pin.

Thank you, God, for tiny things
that creep and crawl.

God made the animals.

Button Animals

1-inch (2.5-cm) craft buttons with four holes

pipe cleaner

tiny wiggle eyes

scissors

1 String a piece of pipe cleaner through one of the top holes of the button for the neck and head of the animal. Make the piece twice as long as you want the neck and head to be. String the piece halfway through and twist the two pieces together to form the neck. It might be an animal with a very long neck like a giraffe, or with a short neck like a cat. Fold the ends of the pipe cleaner down and back for the head, then tip the ends up for ears.

2 String a piece through the top back hole for a tail. Make the piece twice as long as you want the tail to be. Thread it halfway through the hole, then twist the two ends together around the button.

3 Cut two pieces of pipe cleaner for legs. Thread one piece through each hole, then twist the two ends around each other once below the button. Spread the two ends out to form a leg on each side of the button.

4 Glue two tiny wiggle eyes to the head of the button animal.

Make lots of different kinds of animals using different color buttons and pipe cleaners.

Thank you, God, for the animals.

47

God made animals of all kinds.

Spoons Bunny Magnet

you need:

masking tape

white glue

pink pom-pom

two white plastic spoons

two wiggle eyes

yellow yarn

thin pink ribbon

sticky-back magnet

scissors

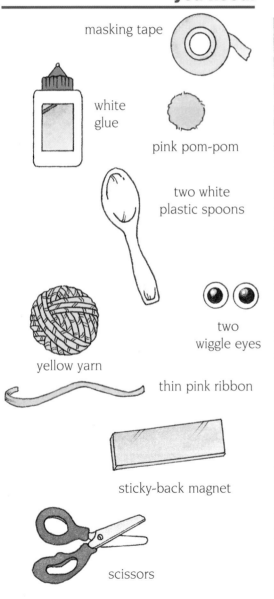

what you do:

1 Put a rolled piece of masking tape, sticky side out, on the right side of the back of one spoon. Put another piece of rolled masking tape in the bowl of the other spoon. Put some glue over the tape and press the tape-covered bowl of one spoon over the tape-covered back of the second spoon. Turn the top spoon slightly so that the two handles form rabbit ears, and the crossed bowls of the spoons form the face.

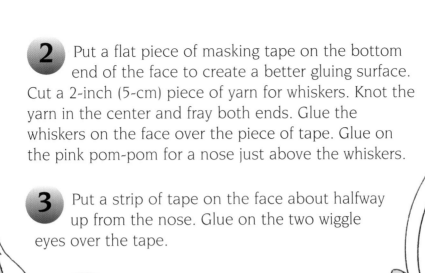

2 Put a flat piece of masking tape on the bottom end of the face to create a better gluing surface. Cut a 2-inch (5-cm) piece of yarn for whiskers. Knot the yarn in the center and fray both ends. Glue the whiskers on the face over the piece of tape. Glue on the pink pom-pom for a nose just above the whiskers.

3 Put a strip of tape on the face about halfway up from the nose. Glue on the two wiggle eyes over the tape.

4 Put a piece of tape just below the two handle ears. Tie a piece of pink ribbon into a bow. Glue the bow over the tape below the ears.

5 Put a piece of sticky-back magnet on the back of the top of each ear.

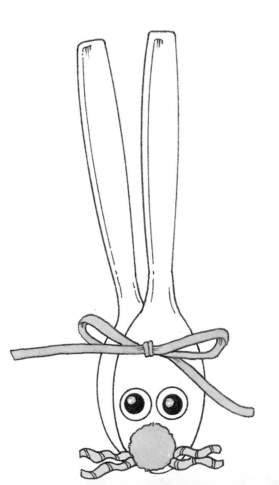

Stick this little bunny on the refrigerator as a reminder to thank God for the animals.

Thank you, God, for making all kinds of animals.

Glove Dog Puppet

you need:

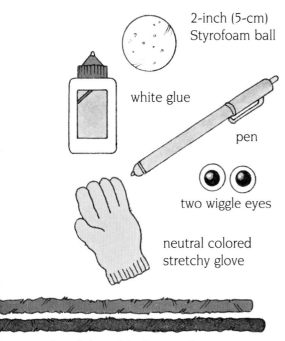

2-inch (5-cm) Styrofoam ball

white glue

pen

two wiggle eyes

neutral colored stretchy glove

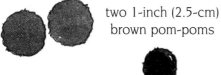

one red and three black pipe cleaners

two 1-inch (2.5-cm) brown pom-poms

1/2-inch (1.3-cm) black pom-pom

masking tape

scissors

what you do:

1 Use the pen to push a hole through the side of the Styrofoam ball. Work at the hole until it is large enough to put the end of your middle finger in. Slip the glove on your hand. Put the Styrofoam ball on the end of your middle finger. The ball will be the head of the dog, and the four fingers of the glove will be the legs.

2 Thread a 12-inch (30-cm) pipe cleaner through the knit fabric just above the cuff of the glove. Twist the two ends of the pipe cleaner together to form the tail.

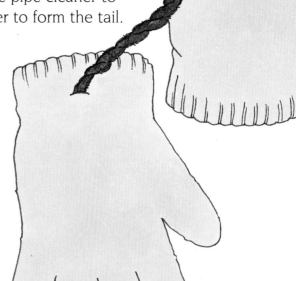

3 Shape the red pipe cleaner into a circle about 1 1/2 inches (3.75 cm) across for a collar for the dog. Remove the head to slip the collar over the middle finger. It should hang loose.

4 Shape two pointed or floppy ears for the dog from the black pipe cleaners. Poke an ear into each side of the head.

5 Put a small piece of masking tape on the back of each wiggle eye to create a better gluing surface. Glue the two eyes on the front of the head.

6 Glue the two larger brown pom-poms on the head below the eyes for the muzzle. Glue the black pom-pom on the end of the muzzle for the nose.

Put your hand in the glove body and secure the head on the end of your finger. Now take the dog for a walk.

Thank you, God, for animals that like to live with people.

God made all
the people.

Row of People

you need:

cardboard egg carton

poster paints in six bright
colors and a paintbrush

poster paints in
six skin tones

12 beads and/or
wiggle eyes

six tiny pom-poms

white
glue

red marker

buttons

yarn bits in
different hair
colors

six 12-inch (30-cm) pipe cleaners

ribbon for bow

masking
tape

scissors

newspaper
to work on

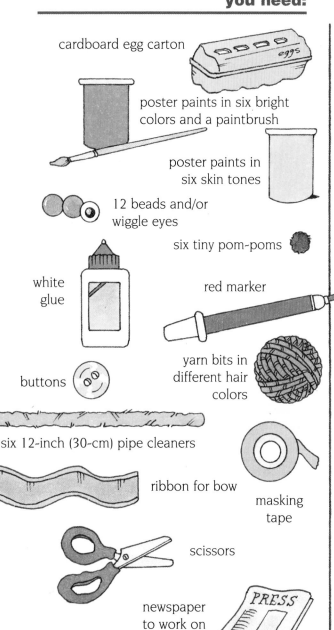

what you do:

1 Cut the lid off the top of the egg
carton. Paint the outside of the lid
for the "people" to sit on.

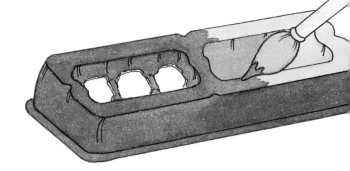

2 Turn the bottom part of the egg carton over. The top row of bumps will
be the heads for the people, and the bottom row the bodies. Paint each bump in
the top row a different skin tone. Paint
each bump in the bottom row a different
bright color.

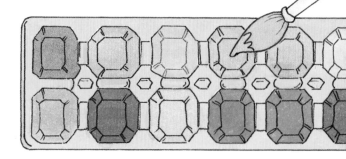

3 Glue two wiggle eyes or beads on each face. Glue on a pom-pom below each pair of eyes for the nose. Use the red marker to give each person a smile. Glue different color yarn bits on the top of each head for hair.

4 Decorate each body by gluing on a bow or button.

5 Fold each of the six pipe cleaners in half to form legs. Bend the ends to make feet. Glue the folded ends of the pipe-cleaner legs along the lid of the egg carton. Use masking tape to hold the legs in place while the glue is drying. Bend the legs down over the front of the carton to make knees.

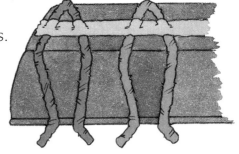

6 Glue the people across the lid of the carton over the legs so that each person has a pair of legs sticking out from the body.

Isn't it amazing how different each person is?

Thank you, God, for all the different people.

God made so many
different people!

Different People
Envelopes Puzzle

what you do:

eight or more used white
envelopes with nothing
written on the back

1 Line up four different envelopes, unwritten-on side up, one below the other. Draw a head on the top envelope. On the second envelope draw the upper body, as a continuation of the first drawing. On the third envelope draw the lower body portion in pants or a skirt. On the last envelope draw the legs and feet.

2 Remove the head envelope and replace it with a fresh one. Draw a different head on this one, but make it line up with the upper body below it. Do the same thing with each of the other envelopes. You can make as many different envelope pieces as you want, making sure each piece lines up with the original drawing.

3 Add details and color all the different parts with markers.

Have fun making lots of different-looking people by trying different combinations of envelope parts.

Thank you, God, for making each of us in your image.

God made you.

Label Necklace

you need:

corrugated cardboard

scissors

markers

stickers

colored vinyl electrical tape

thin ribbon or yarn

hole punch

what you do:

1 Cut a 5- by 7-inch (13- by 18-cm) piece of corrugated cardboard. Snip off the corners at one end to make it look like a tag. Round off all the corners.

2 Use the markers to write, "Made with love by GOD" on one side of the tag. Decorate the tag any way you want using markers and stickers.

3 Use the electrical tape to make a border for the tag.

4 Punch a hole in the center of the end of the tag with the trimmed corners.

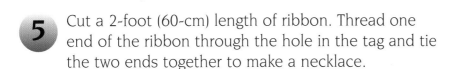

5 Cut a 2-foot (60-cm) length of ribbon. Thread one end of the ribbon through the hole in the tag and tie the two ends together to make a necklace.

You can wear the label as a reminder that you come from God.

Thank you, God, for making me.

God loves the world.

Cross Pin

you need:

eight small gold
safety pins

seed beads in
two colors (make
sure the openings
are large enough
to string on
safety pins)

what you do:

1 Open one safety pin and put on seed beads of one color, then close the safety pin to hold them in place. It will take about eight beads. Because pins can vary, the number of beads needed might vary too, but the idea will still work. Do the same thing with the second safety pin.

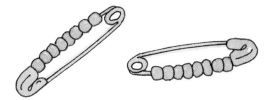

2 On the next four safety pins put on four beads of the same color as the first two safety pins, then one bead of the second color, then three more beads of the first color. Close each safety pin to hold the beads in place.

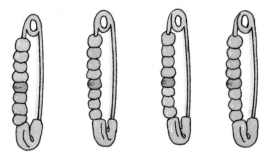

58

3 On the next safety pin put all beads of the second color, then close the safety pin.

4 Open the last safety pin. You are going to thread each safety pin onto the open part of the pin under the head of each closed pin, then slide them around to the back bar of the pin. You need to end up with the beads facing outward when hanging down from the back bar of the holder safety pin. The beaded safety pins must be put on in the following order: 1. safety pin with all first-color beads; 2. and 3. safety pins with seven first-color beads and one second-color bead; 4. safety pin with all second-color beads; 5. and 6. safety pin with seven first-color and one second-color beads; 7. safety pin with all first-color beads. When all the beaded safety pins hang down together, they should form a cross.

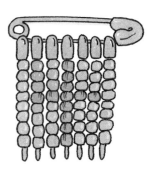

We know that God loves the world, because God gave us Jesus.

Thank you, God, for Jesus.

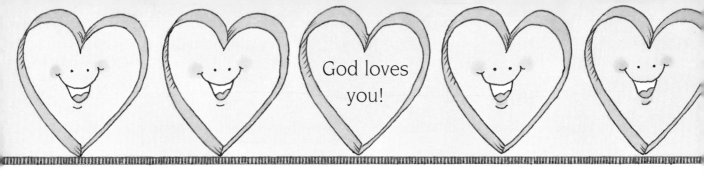
Heart Frame Mask

you need:

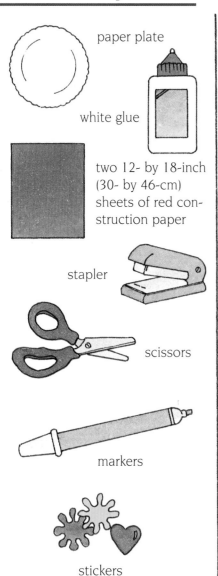

paper plate

white glue

two 12- by 18-inch (30- by 46-cm) sheets of red construction paper

stapler

scissors

markers

stickers

what you do:

 1 Cut out the center part of the paper plate. This will be the base for the mask.

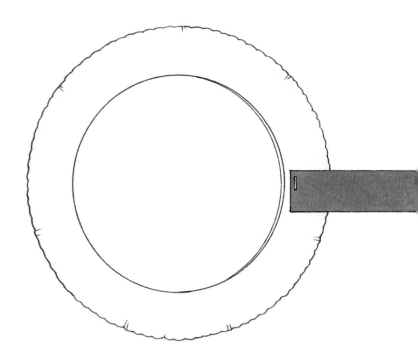

2 Cut a long 1 1/2-inch (3.75-cm)-wide strip from one sheet of the red paper. Staple one end of the strip to the top portion of the edge of the eating side of the paper-plate rim.

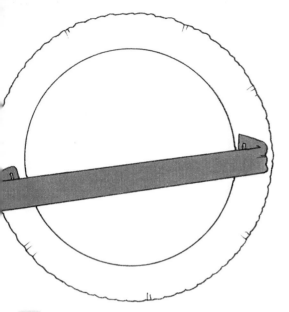

3 Hold the rim up to your face and wrap the rim around your head to make a band to hold the mask in place. Staple the strip to the other side of the rim and trim off any excess paper.

4 Fold the second sheet of paper in half to get a piece that is 9 by 12 inches (23 by 30 cm). Cut half a heart on the fold of the paper, making it as large as the paper will allow. Open up the paper to get a complete heart shape.

5 Place the plate rim on one side of the heart. The plate should not show from the front of the heart. If a tiny part of the plate shows at the top of the heart, just snip off that piece of plate. Trace around the hole in the plate on the heart. Cut the hole out of the heart.

6 Write on the top of the heart, "God Loves . . . " Decorate your heart any way you like, using stickers and/or markers.

7 Glue the heart to the front of the plate rim.

Wear your mask to show everyone that you know that God loves you.

Thank you, God, for loving me.

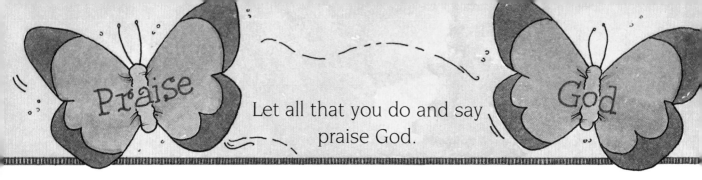

Praise Puppet

you need:

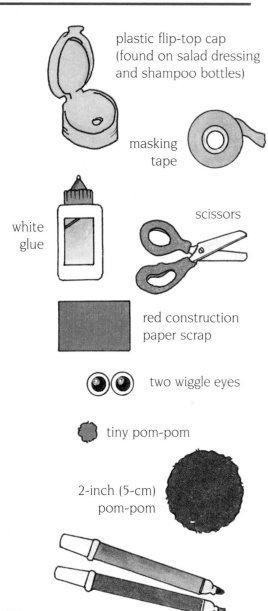

plastic flip-top cap (found on salad dressing and shampoo bottles)

masking tape

white glue

scissors

red construction paper scrap

two wiggle eyes

tiny pom-pom

2-inch (5-cm) pom-pom

markers

what you do:

1 Turn the cap upside-down. The top of the cap will form the bottom jaw of the puppet. Cover the outside of the cap with masking tape. You can use the masking tape shade for the skin color, or use markers to make the skin another color.

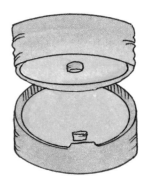

2 Trace around the cap on the red paper. Cut the circle out. Use a marker to write "Praise God" on the circle. Put a piece of masking tape on the inside of the bottom jaw to create a better gluing surface. Glue the circle inside the mouth of the puppet.

Praise GOD

3 Use a marker to draw a smile on the bottom center of the jaw.

4 Put a tiny square of masking tape on the back of each wiggle eye to create a better gluing surface. Glue the eyes to the face, above the open mouth. Glue the tiny pom-pom just below the eyes for the nose.

5 Put a strip or two of masking tape inside the cap, again to create a better gluing surface.

6 Glue one side of the large pom-pom in the cap with most of it sticking out for hair.

This little puppet speaks only to praise God!

God, I praise your name forever and ever. Amen

About the Author and Artist

Twenty-five years as a teacher and director of nursery school programs has given Kathy Ross extensive experience in guiding young children through crafts projects. Among the more than thirty-five craft books she has written are *Crafts For All Seasons*, *Make Yourself a Monster*, *Crafts From Your Favorite Fairy Tales*, and *Crafts From Your Favorite Children's Songs*.

Sharon Lane Holm, a resident of Fairfield, Connecticut, won awards for her work in advertising design before shifting her concentration to children's books. Her recent books include *Sidewalk Games Around the World*, *Happy Birthday, Everywhere!*, and *Happy New Year, Everywhere!* all by Arlene Erlbach, and *Beautiful Bats* by Linda Glaser.

Together, Kathy Ross and Sharon Lane Holm have also created the popular Holiday Crafts for Kids series, Crafts for Kids Who Are Wild About series, as well as two earlier Christian craft books: *Crafts From Your Favorite Bible Stories* and *Crafts for Christian Values*.